HOUSEHOLD HINTS

by
June King

SANTA MONICA PRESS
P.O. Box 1076
Santa Monica, CA 90406-1076
Printed in the United States
All Rights Reserved

Table of Contents

Introduction

How many times have you walked through your house, wishing that things could be more organized? How many times have you thought about the amount of time you could save doing chores if they would just go more smoothly? How many times have you wondered how much money you could save by maintaining things yourself, *before* professional repairmen needed to be called?

If you've wondered about these things, then you're not alone. In fact, people all over the country are finally realizing that they can significantly increase their free time and their savings by putting a little extra effort into organizing their homes.

After reading this book, you'll be delighted to know all the different ways that you can make your chores and daily activities go by more quickly. You will learn, for example, how to rearrange your bathroom in such a way that you and your loved ones can prepare yourselves for the day in a more timely fashion, allowing you to sleep in later or even spend some more quality time together around the breakfast table. You will also discover ingenious ways of reducing your spending, such as saving money on both food and energy bills by keeping your refrigerator and freezer fully stocked!

You might be asking yourself if you are capable of reorganizing your household so drastically as to achieve results like these. But rest assured, the kinds of changes you need to make are so minor that they are well within the reach of anyone. Many of the tasks can be turned into group efforts, bringing your whole family together for fun activities such as garage sales. Isn't it wonderful to know that by working together, your family members can create even more free time to spend with each other?

If you do find yourself needing help, then there are plenty of convenient channels you can go through in order to hire a responsible person. This book will show you how to find the right person for the job, helping you to insure that you can place confidence in your hired help.

Hopefully, once you have finished looking through these pages, you will understand how to turn your household into a better home. You will know how to save both time and money, which can be a reward for the entire family! Good luck!

Chapter 1:
The Kitchen

The kitchen is one of the most important rooms in any household, but unfortunately most people just don't keep it organized. They have to waste precious time every morning while preparing breakfast (we all know *exactly* how it feels to stare at our watches while we scramble through the refrigerator looking for something to eat, just wishing that we had five extra minutes before departing for work). And there is nothing worse than interrupting quality family time because you haven't planned your dinner in advance, and it takes you over an hour to prepare it. Plus, how many hours have you wasted while trying to keep your kitchen clean?

But don't fret! The few, simple tips you will find within this chapter are sure to make your kitchen better organized, more pleasurable in which to spend your time, and more efficient.

APPLIANCES

Fresh Refrigerators

Keeping your refrigerator smelling fresh can be one the biggest nuisances you will ever face in your kitchen. The best way to eliminate such foul smells is to place a few charcoal briquettes on a plate in the refrigerator. When the pieces of charcoal seem to stop working, simply warm them in a frying pan for a few minutes.

Cold is Cheap

Freezers work most efficiently, and therefore least expensively, when they are extremely full. Put as much food in it as you can in order to reduce your energy bill. This might also reduce your grocery bill, as buying in bulk is always cheaper and quicker (you don't have to make as many trips to the store).

Clean Refrigerators
are Happy Refrigerators

Removing dust from beneath your refrigerator is one of the easiest ways to make it last for years and years. You should move it every three months so that you can give it a good

13

cleaning (that pesky dirt really sticks to the bottom!), but don't forget to unplug it to reduce the risk of shock. Doing this will save you a great deal of time and money, as your refrigerator will better regulate its temperature, allowing foods to stay fresh for longer — that means you won't have to go to the grocery store as often!

Soggy Defrosting

Defrosting a freezer can be such a bother if you have to wipe it out. A quicker and easier method is to line the bottom of your freezer with a few absorbent towels. The towels will soak up all the water when you defrost the freezer.

Clean Pipes

We all know that annoying feeling of staring down into a kitchen sink that won't drain. In order to prevent your pipes from clogging up, there are a few simple precautions to take. First, never wash oil or fat down the drain; wait for it to solidify and throw it out instead. Second, brush any pieces of food (even the small crumbs!) into the garbage rather than letting them go down the drain. One of the best ways to get rid of a clog that is already in your drain is to pour a mixture of salt and boiling water into it.

The Amazing Defroster
You Never Knew You Had

Oh no, you just found out that you're going to have guests over for dinner, but you don't have any meat defrosted! What are you going to do? Just whip out your trusty old electric wok or frying pan and put the meat in on a low temperature. Put the lid on, and a few minutes later your meat will start to defrost.

Clean Frying

To keep oil from splashing out of your frying pan and onto your beautiful stove, use a metal strainer or colander as a lid. The oil will stay in, but the hot air will find its way out through the holes.

Microwave Safe?

The microwave is one of the greatest conveniences available in modern kitchens, but sometimes it's hard to tell if your dishes are microwave safe. The best way to test a dish is to put it in the microwave with a measuring cup filled with water. Heat for one minute at the highest power. Check the temperature of each; if the dish is cold and the water hot, then the dish is microwave safe.

Good, Clean Trash

There's nothing quite as stinky as the smell of a dirty garbage disposal, but it's quite simple to make the problem go away. Toss in a few rinds from citrus fruits and turn the disposal on. An even more powerful method is to make a batch of ice cubes with a healthy dose of vinegar in them; pour the cubes down the drain and turn it on. The smell will disappear almost immediately! Before doing this, however, you should test the disposal with one or two cubes, to make sure that it is strong enough.

Golden Brown

The toast is burning! To avoid this early-morning nightmare, make sure that the crumb tray in the bottom of your toaster is kept clean. This will prevent your toast from getting burned, thus saving you quite a bit of time and money every morning.

16

Clean Burning

Cooking with gas is one of the most economical ways to prepare your food. But burners can easily become clogged, thereby decreasing their efficiency and increasing your gas bill (a yellow flame, as opposed to blue, is a sure sign of a clog). To clean them, take a toothbrush and make sure that no dirt is stopping up any of the holes. But never do this with the gas turned on!

Power Out Precautions

If the electricity goes out in your home due to a blackout, then you should make sure to remove all of your appliances from the wall sockets. This will prevent them from shorting out when power returns, as there is usually a strong surge of electricity for the first few seconds.

Smooth Blending

If you have one of those European style blenders (you know, the one with the two whisks that beat into a bowl), then you probably never use it because of the horrible mess it can make. To prevent the whisks from spraying your whole kitchen with batter or any

17

other mixture you are blending, simply apply a small amount of non-stick spray to them. This will ensure that the batter keeps "falling" back into the bowl.

I Didn't Do It!

We all know the feeling. The coffee maker just won't work, no matter what you do. The only thing that anyone will say is, "I didn't do it!" Well before you call the repairman, here are a few things you can check for yourself. Is the fuse blown? Is the outlet at fault (check this by plugging in something that you know works)? Is the appliance plugged into the socket and turned on? Is the plug coming loose from the wire (this one is very important for all you naughty people who unplug things by pulling on the cord, rather than on the plug — don't try to fix this yourself)?

STORAGE

Old Enough to Date

It can become very confusing to try and figure out which of your leftovers are oldest and should be eaten first. This problem can be remedied by a small pieces of paper with the date that you originally cooked the dish written on it. Simply tape the piece of paper to the container in which you're storing the leftover, and *voila*!

Where Did I Put That?

It seems like you can waste hours hunting and poking through a disorganized refrigerator, looking for different food items. To save yourself some time in the future, take one afternoon to completely reorganize your refrigerator. Group all of the similar items in one area. Put the taller ones *behind* the shorter ones, so that you will have no trouble seeing both (I hate it when I can't see what's behind that mayonnaise jar!). Until you have memorized your new plan, you might even want to make a little map or chart for yourself. This might sound silly at first, but in the long run you'll love it.

Fresh and Crispy

Let's face it, vegetables are always best when they are freshest, but there are certain things you can do to increase their storage life. Before you freeze them, most vegetables need to be blanched, and potatoes need to be cooked entirely. Greens will lose most of their crispness once frozen, so they must be cooked before eating.

No More Scratches

It's usually most convenient to stack your dishes and frying pans, as this can save a lot of space. But if you're not careful when reaching for a pan or plate, you can easily scratch the one beneath it. That's why you should try separating each with a disposable foam plate. You might try using paper plates, or even extra strong paper towels, but neither of these will last as long as foam.

Uncanny Idea

You should keep canned foods away from extreme temperatures; don't store them next to the oven, for example. Don't ever open a can of food that has any rust on it — just throw it out, because it might be tainted. Also, when opening a can, if you hear a strong hissing noise, like the sound of steam escaping, then throw it out, because it has definitely gone bad. If you're eating a can of food that has a considerable amount of fat in it, but you want to reduce the fat you intake, then here's a neat idea. Open the can and put it in the refrigerator for about an hour or two. The fat will all solidify, and you can lift it out with a spoon.

Ordered Utensils

Making sense out of your utensil drawers can be a nightmare! Well, here are three tips to make it a little easier for you. First, try buying a rotating tie rack that you can put on the counter, from which you can hang utensils that have holes in their handles, such as ladles and certain knives. Next, put all of your table flatware in a cup or jar on the counter, so that they are within easy reach at mealtime. Finally, to stop any utensils that are in drawers from rattling, try lining the drawer with Styrofoam.

Fish Facts

If you buy fresh fish that has not been frozen, then never freeze it (that would defeat the whole purpose of buying it fresh). It can be stored for about half a day in the refrigerator.

Fill a colander with ice, and put the fish in the ice. Always keep a bowl underneath to catch ice water as it melts and drips through the holes. If you have frozen fish that you want to eat, then put it in a bowl of milk for at least an hour after it has defrosted. This will soften the taste.

Spicy Ideas

Do you remember the beautiful old spice rack your mother used to have? Sometimes it seems like it will take hours to search through such a rack and find the spices you need. A simple idea to make things quicker for you is to place them on the rack alphabetically. If you think that you're not going to use a spice very often, then put it in the refrigerator to keep it fresh.

Strong Glasses

Drinking glasses make wonderful storage containers (for everything from recipes and napkins to utensils and packaged spices). But if you're afraid that your glasses might break easily, then here's a simple way to strengthen them. Place each glass into a pot of water with a little salt in it. Boil the water *very, very* slowly, and the glasses will become stronger.

Screwy Ideas

Foods that come in cardboard boxes or non-resealable bags are easy prey for household pests, bacteria, and even curious pets. As such, it's a good idea to buy a large supply of storage containers with screw-on lids. When not using the jar, the lids make excellent coasters or serving dishes for nuts and snacks.

Safe China

Most people use their china very rarely. If you have kept your china in a closet or cupboard for a long time, then let it sit out for an hour before using it. This will prevent it from being damaged by extremely hot or cold food or drink. In fact, you might not want to store your china away at all, as it is thought that china actually gets stronger the more you use it.

Fresh Desserts

Desserts such as pies can be easily frozen and reheated later. The secret is to keep it looking as fresh and beautiful as when it first came out of the oven. To do this, take an empty pie pan and cover your pie with it. Tape the empty pan in place, and your delicious dessert will not get squashed, even if it gets bumped while in the freezer.

Fresh-Brewed Taste

Gourmet coffee can be very expensive. You can reduce the price by buying it in bulk. To keep it tasting just as fresh as the day you bought it, store the excess coffee in an air-tight container in the freezer.

Tightly Sealed

Even if you store foods in specially made storage containers in your refrigerator, you still might find that foods don't last as long as you want them to. For the most part, this is probably due to lids that are not perfectly air-tight. Cover the top of the container with plastic wrap before screwing the lid in place. This will also keep your refrigerator smelling fresher.

Wonderful Wine

If you like to drink wine every now and then, here are a few tips for storing your wine. Always lay the bottle flat on its side, rather than keeping it upright. This way the wine will coat the bottom of the cork, preventing air from getting in and spoiling it. Once you have drunk the wine, keep the corks and the bottles, as they make excellent storage containers. Not only are they great for liquids, such as oil and vinegar, but you can also fill them with snacks like unpopped popcorn or candy.

Fresher Bread

Don't you hate opening up a bag of bread and finding mold inside? To enjoy your bread longer, leave no more than half a loaf out. The rest should be kept in the freezer. This is especially useful if you buy bread in bulk, which always saves you plenty of money. Once the bread defrosts, it can either be toasted or eaten as is.

Sensible Storage

One of the most important storage tips requires virtually no work at all, just a little common sense. Put the things that you use most often in convenient areas, not at the backs of shelves. Put heavier things, such as pots and pans, closer to the ground, and lighter things, such as napkins, up high. Although bottles are usually quite light, they should still be placed closer to the ground, in order to reduce the risk of shattering if they get knocked over.

Take a Look Around

The fact of the matter is that most people never really look around their kitchen before they start putting things on the shelves. Give yourself a little time, walk around your kitchen and "practice" making your favorite dishes; your most common ingredients (and the cleaning supplies to clean up in the event you drop something) should be located in places that are easy to get to. Be creative! For example, instead of taking up valuable closet space with your broom, why not lean it against the side of your refrigerator in that small space between your counter and refrigerator?

Get into Habits

Let's face it, bad habits are hard to break, and good habits are even harder to form. How many of us really follow the old rule "Clean as you cook?" Here's a way to keep your kitchen organized, even under heavy use. Once you have found the perfect storage areas, using the various methods outlined above, make a chart for yourself to help you memorize everything's location. While you are cooking, simply put each item, such as a spice jar, in a box next to the stove once you are done with it. This will keep your counter space open, and when you're done, you can quickly return everything from the box to its rightful place.

COOKING

Sweet Smelling Onions

Onions make your food smell delicious, but they make your hands smell yucky. The best way to rid your fingers of their scent is first to dab them in a bowl of vinegar. Vinegar far overpowers the smell of onions, and it is much easier to wash out when you are done. The vinegar from your fingers even adds an interesting sharpness to the taste of the onions.

Chlorinated Water

Many communities put small doses of chlorine into their water supplies to ensure the cleanliness of water from the tap. The chlorine is perfectly safe and drinkable, but it often makes the water unappetizing. To rid yourself of this problem, put the water in a large metal bowl and stir it brusquely with a wooden spoon. This motion will force the chlorine gas out of the water. If you have more time, simply leave the water in the bowl for 12 to 24 hours, and the gas will leave by itself.

Fruit Juice Cubes

On a hot summer day, there's nothing like a glass of fruit juice on the rocks. But as the ice begins to melt, it makes your beverage all watery and less tasty. To avoid this problem, simply make ice cubes from your favorite fruit juices. That way, when the ice melts, it will simply increase the amount of beverage in your glass.

Juicy Lemons

Squeezing lemon into your favorite beverage or food is a wonderful way to increase its natural flavors. But lemons can be expensive, and they never seem to have very much juice in them. To get double the amount of juice from your lemon (or any other citrus fruit, for that matter), simply heat it up! Either put it in the microwave for a minute or so, or place it in a pot of hot water. Careful not to burn your hands!

Down the Drain

How many times have you put a bowl on the counter, dropped your ingredients into the bowl, and started mixing it with a spoon, only to find your mixture spilling everywhere? To prevent this sloppy situation, and the time that you have to spend cleaning it up, place the bowl in the sink. That way, there's no mess caused by any spills.

Easy Greasy

Always keep the paper wrapping that comes with a pat of butter or margarine. Whenever a recipe calls for you to grease a pan, simply wipe the wrapper over the pan. That way, there's less waste.

Good Grating

Freshly grated cheeses and vegetables are so much more appetizing and appealing than pre-grated foods. But sometimes it can be difficult to grate food yourself. To make this task easier, grate vegetables and cheeses as soon as you remove them from the refrigerator, so they will be a little firmer. When you're done grating, brush any particles of food out of the holes with a basting brush; that way, there's no waste.

Tender Victuals

Many recipes with beef or pork call for you to tenderize the meat. There are two great ways for you to do this. First, take the back of a clever (or any other heavy utensil) and hammer it against the meat. Or second, if the meat is cut thin, marinate it in a bowl filled with either lemon juice or wine vinegar. Tenderizing by marinating also brings out and enhances the flavor of your dishes.

Smells Fishy

Let's face it, as delicious as sea food may be, raw fish makes your hands smell yucky! To prevent the smell from sticking to your fingers while you prepare your seafood, keep the fish in ice water. Extremely cold fish will still smell a little, but far less than if the fish gets warm.

Turkey Dinner

Everyone seems to think that carving a turkey is difficult, but it's actually quite simple, as long as you follow these directions. To remove white meat, cut directly downwards until you hit bone, using the breastbone as a guide. Then turn the knife horizontal and cut outwards. Repeat for the other side. You will then have two succulent turkey breasts, which can easily be sliced on a cutting board. To remove legs and wings, pull the appendage away from the body and hunt for the joint with the tip of your knife. When you finally find the cartilage, your knife should be able to cut through it without any problem whatsoever.

Muffin Trick

English muffins are so yummy, and they certainly make a nice change from toast, but sometimes they stick inside the toaster. A great way to rid yourself of this sticky situation is to make an "axle" through the center of the muffin with a toothpick. Place the muffin in the toaster, until it reaches the axle. Toast one half of your muffin "wheel," then pull it out, rotate it around the axle, and then toast the other half. Never, *never*, use anything metal as your axle (see the chapter on safety)!

Perky Idea

Remember the old percolator your mother gave you as a wedding present? Thanks to those new high tech coffee brewers, you probably don't use it much anymore. But percolators work so well for things other than coffee. Why not use it to boil vegetables or even hot dogs?

Easy on the Oil

A lot of today's health conscious recipes call for you to use small amounts of oil when frying, but it can be very difficult (not to mention messy) to measure out the proper amount. You should save your dish washing detergent bottles once they are empty as they make it simple to dispense small dabs of oil! This really makes it easy to keep your hands and countertops clean when cooking with oil.

Efficient Shopping

If you plan well before going shopping for groceries, then you can cut down both the time and money you spend. First, keep all of the coupons that you collect throughout the week in one place. When you make your grocery list, check it against the coupons you have to see if you can find discounts on what you're going to buy. Second, when writing down your list, visualize to yourself the layout of the grocery store where you usually shop. That way, you can get each item in order from the top of the list to the bottom, without forgetting anything or running backwards and forwards in the supermarket.

Chapter II:
The Bathroom

Like the kitchen, the bathroom is one of the most important rooms in your house. But for some reason, people are almost afraid of it, as if plumbing is an ancient secret only comprehensible to a select few. There are probably dozens of simple things that you can do right now to make your bathroom better organized and more efficient. This chapter will instruct you on how to do everything from keeping counter space clean to taking some of the stress out of your morning schedule.

This chapter also includes a few basic hints on plumbing and repairs. Do not be frightened about these repairs. If you do not feel confident in performing them yourself, then by all means call a plumber. They are included in the chapter only for those who wish to save some money by doing some very simple work without seeking help from a professional.

STORAGE

Hanging Baskets

Most bathrooms are small and cluttered, with hardly enough space for one person's belongings, let alone for a whole family's. A good way to solve this problem is to place hooks on the ceiling from which you can hang baskets (much like some flowers are attached to the ceiling) where you can put your toiletries.

Shoe Boxes Aren't Just for Shoes

Remember how you used to keep your favorite toys in shoe boxes when you were a kid? Well, why did you ever stop using shoe boxes for storage? They're sturdy and they come in practical sizes, perfect for holding hairbrushes, combs, spray cans, makeup, toothbrushes and toothpaste. Each member of your family can have his or her own box, and there will never again be any confusion about which item belongs to whom. And as long as you don't lose the lid, then the shoe box can be tucked away almost anywhere in the bathroom without dirtying or damaging the things inside.

Make Room for Medicine

Believe it or not, the bathroom is the worst place to keep your medicines. Prescription and non-prescription drugs need to be kept in very stable environments, and the temperature and humidity fluctuates more in the bathroom (due to showers and baths) than in any other room in the house. By putting your medicines in a safe place away from kids in the kitchen or bedroom, then you will clear valuable shelf space for your toiletries.

Handy Loops

For some reason, the people who design bathrooms always seem to forget that children need things placed at lower heights. Young kids very often can't reach towel racks, making it a difficult chore for their parents to clean up after them everyday. Why not buy one of those towel rings, and attach it to the wall at a height that is comfortable for your child?

A Naughty No-No

The worst place in the bathroom to store anything is on the tank of your toilet. Not only is their a serious risk that something will fall into the toilet bowl if you leave the seat up, but it also makes it a difficult chore to open up the tank if you need to adjust the plunger or float bowl inside.

Mirror, Mirror

Most mirrors in bathrooms just aren't big enough for more than one person to look at him or herself at a time. If you find that several of your family members need the mirror at once (for shaving, applying makeup, brushing their hair, etc.) then you should buy a full-length mirror and attach it to the wall *horizontally*, so that people can stand next to each other. Better yet, to cut down traffic in the bathroom, why not do any personal chores that do not require a sink, such as applying makeup, in the mirror in your bedroom instead? That way, each person will spend less time in the bathroom, and many items, such as hairbrushes, can be stored in bedrooms, thereby increasing counter space.

Sticky Situation

Many medicine cabinets have shelves made out of glass. These shelves can be quite dangerous in two ways. First, their front edges are sometimes extremely sharp. And second, items can be easily knocked from them. If you line the shelves with Styrofoam, such as from meat packaging at a grocery store, then you will rid yourself of both problems. Not only will the sharp edges be covered, but the Styrofoam will also create a considerable amount of friction, "sticking" your items to the shelves. But don't forget to wash the Styrofoam thoroughly before using it for this purpose.

Tidy Cords
One of the biggest problems with storing things in bathrooms is that power cords from hairdryers and other such appliances get easily tangled. Even worse, these cords can dangle and come into contact with water, which can be very dangerous. To keep your cords neatly wound, and therefore easier to store, simply wind them up and insert them into a used toilet paper tube.

Cotton Dispenser
If you need a place to put your cotton balls, then why not try stuffing them into empty tissue boxes? That way you won't have to hide an ugly plastic bag (the type of packag-

ing in which cotton balls usually come) in your bathroom closet, where it will take up valuable space. A tissue box is more than pretty enough to leave in full view.

Secret Hangers

Many people like to hang their clothes to dry from the shower curtain rod, but this can be an unpleasant sight for guests. If you attach several hooks to the inside of your shower curtain, however, then you can hang clothes from these and no one will ever see them! Just make sure to place them high enough on the curtain so that you won't accidentally brush against them and hurt yourself while taking a shower.

Shoe Shine

A good way to keep your bathroom counters shiny and free of clutter is to invest in one of those shoe bags in which 10 or 12 pairs of shoes can fit in their own individual pouch. Shoe bags are very cheap, and you can put just about anything in them, from cans of hair spray to toothbrushes to cleaning supplies. You can even hang them inside doors so that guests won't notice them.

To Each His Own

Most households have more than one bathroom, so why does everyone always wait to get into the same one each morning? Instead of having your family members wait in line, why don't you just keep everyone's toiletries in different bathrooms? That way, since you don't have to wait for each other and organize yourself around each other's schedules, you might be able to get a few more minutes of sleep in the morning!

DAY-TO-DAY CARE AND PLUMBING

Drip, Drip

While a leaking faucet certainly isn't as complicated to fix as most people believe, here's a neat little idea to rid yourself of the problem for a day or two, before the plumber arrives. Wet a washcloth and squeeze out the excess moisture, so that it is damp but not sopping. Then place the washcloth over the drain where the dripping occurs. This will not solve the problem, but it will get rid of the irritating sound of dripping water. Whenever the washcloth gets saturated with water, simply wring it out and replace it under the leaky faucet.

Dry Porcelain

Don't you hate it when the porcelain fixtures in your bathroom get covered in condensed moisture after you have a hot shower, dripping water all over the floor? Not only can this be a nuisance to dry, but it can also be quite dangerous, as tile floors can become very slippery. In order to minimize this problem, try rubbing some wax on the porcelain at least four times a year.

Clear Mirrors

The mirror in your bathroom always fogs up after you've had a shower, but you can easily solve this by pointing your blow dryer at it and letting the hot air evaporate the moisture. An even better way is to simply drape a towel across it while you bathe. That way, you don't waste any electricity, and the towel is within easy reach.

Clogged Toilets

When a toilet gets clogged, you should usually be able to fix it yourself, saving the high expense of calling a plumber. There are three simple steps to follow. First, scoop some of the water out of the bowl with a bucket. Next, get a plunger and put it as far into the bowl as you can, covering the hole entirely. Pump it vigorously for a few minutes. Repeat every half hour. Finally, if the clog still doesn't come loose, then unwind a toilet snake into the drain and try to pull out the clog. Only after trying these steps should you call a plumber. Never pour any kind of liquid clog remover into a toilet, as a noxious gas could be released.

Clean Shower Heads

Shower heads that are partially obstructed due to a build up of dirt and grime increase your water consumption, as you have to take longer showers to get just as clean. Shower heads are quite simple devices, and they can be removed and taken apart with a few common tools. Place the pieces in an acidic liquid such as vinegar, and leave them overnight. The next day, most of the build-up should be gone, making your shower head more cost efficient.

Clogged Shower Drains

Showers, unlike kitchen sinks, usually tend to get clogged by the same thing over and over again: hair! The following procedure should help you unclog your pipe. Start by pouring a cup of baking soda into the pipe. After a few minutes, add a cup of vinegar. Finally, a few minutes later, add about a half-gallon of very hot (perhaps even boiling) water.

Heavy Curtains

In your bathroom, does your shower curtain seem to get sucked in toward you whenever you turn the water on? This is due to the sudden change in pressure within your shower caused by the force of the water. Try sewing some heavy coins or other small weights into the hem of the curtain.

Soap Dish Mounting

Has your soap dish fallen off the wall long ago, but you just haven't gotten around to fixing it? You should do it as soon as possible, so you can finally remove that bar of soap from the counter around the sink (every bit of storage space counts). Such dishes are very easy to put back on the wall, thanks to the lines of new cements that are now available in hardware stores. You can apply these cements directly to the tiles on your bathroom wall, rather than having to pry the tile off first. Simply follow the directions on the package.

Straight as an Arrow

Some shower heads just don't spray the water in a straight, even line. This can get annoying, as you have to "chase" the water around the tub, wasting precious money (on a needlessly expensive utility bill) and time. If you're not handy with tools, and don't think you can truly fix the problem without calling a plumber, then try this little trick. Cut a hole in the tip of a conical waxed paper cup, and attach the cup to the shower head with a rubber band. The cup will have to be replaced quite frequently, but the water will come out straight. If you can find a more durable item with a small hole in it, such as the top of a soda bottle, then so much the better, as it won't have to be replaced so often. Remember not to turn your water up too high, as the force could dislodge the cup.

Easy Opening

Does your medicine cabinet have two sliding doors in front that overlap each other? You've probably noticed that these doors can get stuck in their runners, and it always seems to happen in the morning when you are late for work. The solution to this problem is simple. Using a cotton swab, simply apply a conservative amount of petroleum jelly to the runners. This technique will also work well with your shower, if you have the glass doors that rest in runners.

Sealed Tight

Does it seem like all the grout that should be sealing your bathtub in place is crumbling off? The reason for this is that conventional grout loses its strength over the years when it comes into contact with water. It is an extremely simple job to regrout your bathtub using one of the new high-tech silicone sealants that are available at any hardware store. Simply follow the directions on the tube, and *voila*! Your bathroom will instantly look better.

Dog Bath

If you have a dog, then you know how difficult it can be to bathe one. Not only do they like to jump around, but they leave trails of water and damp hair everywhere. Well here's a little tip to help make your chore a little quicker and easier. In order to prevent your pet's hair from going down the drain, and almost certainly causing a clog, put a piece of steel wool over the drain in place of your usual hair catcher. It will be much more effective!

Fun in the Tub

Bathing your youngster can go much more quickly and smoothly if he or she is entertained. There are all sorts of things you can do to make bath time more fun. Why not save an old egg carton for your child to use as a boat, or add a few soapy bubbles? You can make inexpensive floating toys out of just about anything that you would normally throw out, such as soda bottles. When your child is having fun, he or she won't struggle so much with you, and that way the bath will be completed much more quickly. Additionally, there won't be nearly as much mess to clean up afterwards.

Chapter III: Other Rooms

This chapter is designed to help you make the remainder of your house more organized. Not only will you learn to get up and out of bed more quickly each morning, but you will also discover all the storage space you never realized you had. For those of you wanting to turn one of your extra rooms into an office, you'll learn everything you need to know to get going.

Most of these tips require very few tools and virtually no experience at handiwork, so don't be afraid to try something new. But if you don't feel comfortable picking up a screwdriver, then perhaps you can ask one of your friends to do it for you. Just show them the instructions outlined below.

Much of the information which follows concerns the closets found throughout your house. Following these suggestions, you can make rooms such as the bedroom, family room, living room, and dining room far more organized.

STORAGE

Pick the Right Color

The best thing you can do in order to make your closet appear brighter, which is virtually essential for everything to be neat and properly organized, is to paint it the correct color. Most closets are painted white, which is good, but they are usually painted with a matte paint. Repaint the interior of your closet with a glossy paint, and it will seem to shine! If two siblings use a single closet, then why not paint each half a different color in order to help them keep their belongings separate?

Useful Luggage

Most people have their suitcases tucked away in the backs of their closets, just wasting precious storage space. They don't want to put their expensive luggage in the garage, basement, or attic, for fear that some rodents might start nibbling on it. You might as well put your suitcase to good use then! Store things inside of it that you don't use everyday. For example, during the summer, why not keep your winter clothes inside it? That way both your suitcases and the clothes within them will be kept perfectly safe.

Keep that Desk Neat

Utensil organizing trays are so useful in the kitchen, so why not use them elsewhere too? They fit perfectly into most desk drawers, and they can easily turn a random pile of odds and ends into a well ordered inventory of supplies. While most adults may be able to keep their home office desks tidy, chores like this are particularly difficult for youngsters, and these trays will certainly help a lot.

Makeshift Furniture

When we were young, we always used to look for creative solutions to a problem, so why don't we do that anymore? If you don't have enough money to furnish your office with *real* furniture from an office supply store, then why not make some yourself? Sturdy cardboard boxes make excellent filing cabinets, for example. Simply divide the boxes into sections for each letter of the alphabet using appropriately marked pieces of paper, and slide your files in! While a desk can't be made out of cardboard, it can be made from cinder blocks and wood. You won't even need any real assembly to build your desk, either; simply stack the bricks up to the correct height (I suggest making a solid leg on either side, rather than a pedestal at each corner) and lay the plank of wood on top. Your desk will probably cost less than twenty dollars!

Closed Curtains

Do you have one of those closets in your bedroom that is so shallow it doesn't even have a closet door? This problem can be rectified by simply hanging a curtain in front of the open closet. Not only will your clothing finally have the privacy it deserves, but you will also have to do laundry less frequently, as dust will not enter the closet so easily.

Create a System

As with your refrigerator, your closet can be a nightmare to keep organized. Why not do yourself a favor and create a system, so that you memorize where everything should go? For example, put all your tops on one side, and all your bottoms on the other. Make sure that your system is sensible; put shoes at the bottom and hats on the top shelf, and not vice versa. In order to help you memorize the locations, make a chart for yourself and tape it to the inside of your closet door. Within a few days, you won't even need the chart anymore.

Home Office Shelves

If you have an empty bedroom that you want to use as a home office, then don't clutter up the floor space by buying a new book shelf. Chances are the closet in the room will be empty, as no clothes will be kept there, so why not turn the closet into a bookcase? Simply add some shelves, and *voila*!

Soap and Socks

Here are two little tricks to help you out in your closets. First, the best way to hang mothballs in your closet is to put them inside a sock taped to the wall. Second, to keep your clothes smelling fresh and eliminate the smell of mothballs, keep an open bar of soap in the closet. A good alternative to this is to put some cinnamon sticks and bay leaves inside your closet.

No More Cling

Static cling can threaten even the best organized closets, making different garments stick together so that you can't see them all, and destroying the order that you have worked so hard to maintain. But you can eliminate this problem with a little dab of hand lotion.

Apply the lotion very conservatively to your garments, massaging it in until the tacky feeling has disappeared, and your clothes will separate nicely.

Dining Room Desk

If you don't have a room in the house that you can use just as an office, and you don't have the money to move into a bigger house, then why not use the dining room? Dining room tables are often bigger than most of the desks you can buy at office supply stores. Instead of buying filing cabinets, just put your paperwork in the drawers and shelves of your cutlery holders. That way, no one will ever know that your dining room is doubling as an office.

Making Files

If you're starting a filing cabinet for yourself for the first time, then the procedure can be somewhat confusing. The following hints should make it a little easier. Once you have accumulated all of your documents, see if any of them can be thrown out (there's no need to file unimportant items). Then pick up the first document, decide what category it belongs to, make a file for that category, and insert the document. The category is some-what arbitrary, and is really more for your convenience in remembering where a document is located; for example, a check with which you made your monthly mortgage payment could go under *House, Home Payments, Mortgage, Monthly Payments,* etc. Then pick up the next document and decide what category it belongs to. If it belongs in the same category, then add it to the first file in chronological order, but if it is a new category, then make a new file. Remember to be consistent (i.e. always put mortgage payments in the same file).

Quick Tricks

Always put empty hangers in the same place on the rod (not the same place where the item of clothing was found), so that you always know where to find them. Also, always place hangers on the rod so that the hooks face the back wall of the closet. That way you won't have to struggle to remove them.

MAKING YOUR BED

Adults

Making your bed can be one of the worst chores of the day, but you have to do it each and every morning. But here are a few tips to make it go faster. First, always keep matching top sheets and bottom sheets together, so that you won't have to rifle through the closet looking for them. Second, make marks on each of your bottom sheets, top sheets, and comforters where they meet the four corners of the bed. That way, you can always line up the different layers perfectly. The mark can be sewn on or drawn on. Lastly, if you're in a real hurry, don't be afraid to leave your bed unmade and pat down the comforter neatly over it; you can always make it when you come home from work later in the day.

Kids

You should definitely teach your kids to start making their beds at a young age, as this will help build their sense of responsibility. But tucking in top sheets and bottom sheets and comforters can be very difficult. That's why a simple quilt can be a better alternative; your kids will learn that making a bed can be quick and easy, and there is no excuse for not doing it.

BASIC REPAIRS
AND DAY-TO-DAY MAINTENANCE

Sticky Situation

Don't you hate it when you're late and trying to rifle through your closet for the outfit you want to wear, but the hangers keep getting stuck on the rod? You can make this problem disappear from your life with a dab of floor wax or furniture polish. When the hangers start sticking again, simply reapply the lubricant.

Smelly Closets

Closets usually smell if they aren't well ventilated. If your closet doesn't have a ventilation duct inside it, then you should leave the doors open overnight (when no guests will be over to see this messy sight). Put some baking soda on the carpet for freshness, and you might even want to tape the wrapper of a scented bar of soap to the wall. Spicy scents are especially good, as they also keep mosquitoes out. It is very important to keep your closet smelling fresh, or your clothes could absorb some foul odors, requiring you to wash them even if you have not worn them.

Screwy Ties

Tie racks that you find in department stores tend to be quite expensive. Instead of spending your money on such an item, why not build one yourself? All you need to do is take some long wood screws and screw them about a quarter-inch into a piece of wood. Arrange the screws in such a way that they form a nice, straight row. Get a piece of wood long enough to hold about ten screws at intervals of a few inches. When you are done, simply hang your ties from the screws.

Doors that Squeak and Creak

There's nothing more aggravating than a closet or hallway door that squeaks, but for some reason you always put off attending to it. Well here's the easiest way to fix it. Go down to a hardware store and ask the manager to help you find silicone lubricant. One or two dabs or sprays of this will take care of that pesky hinge that has annoyed you for so long.

Wet Closets

Sometimes an undue amount of humidity builds up within your closets, which can ultimately damage your clothing. Such a problem may need to be attended to by a professional, but you can give it a shot yourself. The idea is to fill the closet with dry air. You can accomplish this with either a dehumidifier or, if you don't own one of these, a vacuum cleaner set on reverse.

Drawers that Stick

If your desk drawers are getting stuck, then you probably have to force them open with all your might. This destroys all of your attempts at being organized, as everything within the drawer slops around. To solve this problem, remove the drawer. Take a piece of coarse sandpaper (sandpaper comes in varying grades, from coarse to fine) and sand down the sides of the drawer a bit. Then take some floor wax and work it into the bottom. Be careful not to use too much, however, or one tug will make your drawer fly right out of the desk.

Rope Trick

Sometimes you just can't find enough space in your closet, no matter how hard you try. Here's a simple way of solving the problem without having to resort to major changes to the closet. Buy a long spool of strong cord. Cut sections of cord from the spool that are about two feet long. Remove all the hangers from your closet. Tie the cord to the neck of one hanger, making the knot just a few inches from the end. You should then have over a foot of cord coming from this hanger. Tie two more hangers to the cord at equal intervals. Then put the top hanger of each set of three back on the rod, allowing the other two to hang down. Once you put all your clothes back on their hangers, your closet will seem only about one-third full!

Just the Right Height

If you want your child to learn to put on his or her own clothing, then you have to lower the rod so that he or she can reach the hangers. If you're not handy enough to lower the rod, then simply buy another rod (or even a broom handle) and secure it at both ends with strong cords to the original rod, so that the new one dangles below it. Cut the cords to the appropriate length so that your child can reach this rod without having to stretch. Then put all the hangers on this "hanging rod."

Clear Windows

There's nothing as nice as being able to wake up in the morning and look at the beautiful snowy landscape outside. But if jack frost has been nipping at your window, then you won't have much of a view. Simply open the window, apply some rubbing alcohol to the outside, and wipe it off with loosely crumpled newspaper. Incidentally, loosely crumpled newspaper is always the best thing to clean your windows with, as it leaves no streaks or smudges.

Less Scratchy

If you have an office at home where you greet clients or associates, then your office furniture must look very respectable. To remove small scratches from fine wood desks and chairs, mix together a teaspoon of mineral oil and a tablespoon of mashed pecans. Apply the mixture to the scratch, and buff until the scratch is no longer noticeable. This will not eliminate larger and deeper scratches, but it does make them more difficult to see.

Chapter IV:
Garage and Yard

If you're like most people, then your garage has become a place where you almost fear to go. So many year's worth of odds and ends that don't really belong in any other room have piled up so high that you can barely walk through the garage, let alone park your car inside of it at night. Well, this is the chapter you've been waiting for. You'll learn to tame the savage beast that your once clean garage has become!

Next, you'll discover how to take care of your possessions outside of your house, including some basic hints about keeping your lawn beautiful. If you happen to have a pool, then you'll probably benefit from the advice you'll read here. And there's also a few words about your home's exterior.

ORGANIZING YOUR GARAGE

Hold a Garage or Yard Sale

Let's face it, you don't need or want half the things in your garage, so why not participate in an American tradition and hold a garage or yard sale? If you don't try to make too much of a profit, then you'll probably be able to sell well over half of the junk that is littering your floor. You'll be on the road to a more organized garage in no time!

Use the Walls

The key to organizing a garage is getting everything off the floor. Almost anything that you keep in your garage can be suspended on the wall. All power tools should be kept on a peg board screwed into the wall. All sports equipment, such as kids' soccer nets, should be fastened to the wall with special hooks, or even hung from the rafters with durable cord (if the rafters are tall enough, because you don't want to scrape the roof of your car by mistake). Put the things that you use most often close to the ground, and those that are used less frequently higher up.

Shoe Bags

As in other areas of your home, shoe bags are great ways to organize the garage. Hang several of them up in different areas, so that different types of items don't get mixed up. For example, hang one near your work bench to organize tools and gloves. Hang another near your lawn mower to organize gardening supplies such as work boots and small spades.

Parking Spaces

A garage is a room shared by everyone in the family, so why not assign everyone his or her own space? Mom's car should be parked on the left, Dad's car on the right, Junior's bicycle in this corner, the snow tractor in that corner. You should even spray paint the lines for the different "parking spaces," so that no one accidentally intrudes on anyone else's area. This idea is especially good for people who have trouble remembering plans. Just as creating a small chart for the closet in your bedroom helps you remember where everything goes, so will painting these lines remind you how to organize your garage.

Garbage Cans

Almost everyone has more garbage cans than they need, so why waste valuable space? Take any that you are not using and clean them thoroughly with soap and a hose. Once they have dried, line them with a strong garbage bag or a cloth sack and store various items in them. They're especially good for things like hoses and electrical cords which can be difficult to wind up neatly.

Inventory

No matter how organized you are, you are always going to have a few boxes filled with stuff in the garage. But even this can be ordered. Make sure that similar items are found in the same box. Then make an inventory list of the contents and staple it to the side of the box that is in plain view.

No More Oil

Even a well organized garage seems to be plagued by the problem of oil that has dripped from your car onto the ground. The magic ingredient to make such stains disappear is cat box litter. Pour the litter very liberally over the stain, and allow it to sit for a few hours. Then scrub it in with all your might, using a brick or some other heavy and coarse object. Finally, brush away the litter, and *voila*! Don't forget to get your car looked at, because the leak might be serious.

Open and Shut Case

Cracked paint on garage doors is not only unsightly, but it can also cause considerable damage as well. Paint prevents humidity from swelling the wood in the summertime. If your door swells too much, then it could get stuck, and you could break it very easily while trying to open it. Painting a garage door shouldn't take more than a single day, and it is well worth the investment to increase the beauty and durability of the home in which you live.

Now that You can Park Your Car . . .

Once your garage is well ordered enough for you to be able to bring your car back in, you can make the difficult task of parking a little easier with the following idea. Attach a tennis ball to the end of a long piece of cord. Hang the cord from the ceiling of your garage, about a foot from the back wall. Adjust the length of the cord so that the tennis ball is just below the height of the hood of your car. That way, whenever you park, you know you are far enough in when you nudge against the ball.

Future Sales

If your first garage sale was a success, you'll probably have more in the future. But don't allow your garage to accumulate junk like it did before. Instead, whenever you think that you might not want an item anymore, put it in a special box marked "Garage Sale." Once you have accumulated four or five boxes, have another sale.

Soft Landings

If you like to use your power tools in the workshop in your garage, then you've probably felt your heart sink as you accidentally drop one of them into the hard cement ground below. You think to yourself of all the money you've wasted because of your absent-mindedness. The solution to this problem is so simple that you've probably never even thought of it before: put a layer of foam padding on the floor!

WORKING IN YOUR YARD

Slippery Snow Shovel

One of the worst parts about digging the snow out of your driveway is that it keeps sticking to your shovel. Often, you spend just as much time trying to loosen it from your shovel as you do removing it from the driveway. An easy way to solve this problem is to coat your shovel with a silicone lubricant at the beginning of each season. The snow will literally slide off.

Taped Handles

Gardening tools and winter shovels can get lost outside very easily if you're not careful. You can waste hours trying to find them in your yard. To save yourself a lot of time, wrap the handles in coarse, brightly colored tape. This tape will not only make the tool stand out against a green lawn or white snow, but it will also make the handles "grippier."

Hot and Cold Trees

Did you ever think that the way you landscape your yard could possibly affect your utility bills? It may sound silly, but by properly arranging trees, you can make a drastic difference. Plant deciduous trees near your windows; their leaves will keep your interiors shady during summer, but plenty of light will strike your windows when their leaves haven fallen in the winter. Use perennial trees, such as pine trees, as wind screens. Plant them in such a way as to "catch" the wind before it strikes your house!

Delightful Herbs

If your garlic is too old for you to eat, then here's a way to get the most out of it. Fresh garlic is a wonderful way to season your dishes, and it is very easy to grow. Just put the old garlic in a pot in a sunny area, and water it regularly, and *voila*! Your whole family will appreciate the fresh flavor.

All Tied Up

Climbing vines are one of the most beautiful plants with which to adorn your yard, and they are perfect for increasing your privacy. But sometimes, especially when they're young, it can be very difficult for you to keep them tied to their stakes. One of the best ways of doing this is using the green twist ties that come with garbage bags. Since they're green, they virtually disappear in the vine's leaves.

CARING FOR SWIMMING POOLS

Help Out Your Yard

If you only want a shallow pool, such as a pool in which you can swim laps, then here's an interesting way to help out the rest of your yard. By painting the bottom of the pool a dark color like green, instead of the usual light blue, sunlight will reflect off the top of the water. This will help all of the plants in your yard to grow!

Two Toys in One

Put your little one's wading pool inside the sand box you have already built. By smoothing the sand down, you're assuring the pool a snug and safe place to rest, much as professionals do when they build real pools. Moreover, you won't be damaging or taking up an extra portion of your yard. Never leave your child unattended while in a pool!

Heavy Duty

Those wading pools may be small, but they're sure heavy once you've filled them with water! They also seem to get dirty so quickly. To prevent this and save yourself the hassle of having to empty out the water every few days, just keep a bucket of clean water next to the pool. Make your kids clean their feet, hands, and any other dirty places before getting in. This trick works for adult pools too (there's no reason why grown ups shouldn't have to follow the same rules as kids!).

Pool Shed

There's nothing more annoying than seeing your beautiful carpet get muddied by people running in from the pool. An easy way to solve this problem is by erecting an inexpensive metal shack, or even a tent, as a pool shed. Swimmers can dry off and change in it. If you're really handy, then you might want to create a nice shower to wash off the chlorine by hanging a garden hose from a tall rod.

No More Ear Aches

Here's a great little tip that won't help you care for your pool, but it certainly will help you enjoy it even more. If you're prone to those ear aches that so many people get when swimming in chlorinated pools, then dab your ears with a bit of baby oil a few moments prior to jumping in. This oil will lubricate your ears so well that almost no water will get stuck inside!

CARING FOR THE EXTERIOR OF YOUR HOME

Painting Your House

You might think that the best way to beautify your home is by painting it, but you're wrong. In fact, if you paint your house more than once every four or five years, you could be doing serious damage. If you paint this frequently, then the layer of paint gets too thick and becomes brittle; as such, it can crack more easily, allowing the elements to get at the bare wood underneath. The best way to keep your paint looking beautiful for years is to paint less frequently, but apply three coats instead of the usual two. When the paint starts to look a little dirty, scrub it with warm water and an industrial soap that won't damage paint. This

78

is also the perfect way to keep vinyl siding looking new.

Proper Painting

Anyone who has ever painted their house before knows the sight of a paint can with paint that has dripped all down its side. This creates a huge mess in the garage, which is where everyone in the entire world seems to store their half-used cans of paint. This is caused by blotting the paint brush against the rim of the can. To prevent this from happening, simply drill a few holes in the "lip" of the rim which fills up with paint and overflows; any time you blot your brush, the paint will drip back into the can. Since your paint will be permanently exposed to air, you must cover the top of the can very tightly with aluminum foil to prevent it from drying out.

Gutter Gadgets

If you live in an area where the trees shed their leaves each autumn, then you're probably familiar with the problem of dead leaves clogging up your gutter. This problem can lead to serious damage to the down spout, not to mention the water damage the side of your house can receive if the gutter overflows. A great way to prevent this is to use a leaf strainer, an ingenious little gadget that fits at the top of your down spout. But remember to clean the strainer fairly regularly, as it will be useless if you allow it to get clogged up with leaves.

Shuffling Windows

A loose window can pose some serious problems to the homeowner—especially on a nice, sunny day. If not fixed, you will eventually be unable to keep the window open. Who wants to sit inside a house with the windows shut on a beautiful spring day? Solving this problem, however, is a snap. To keep it open, simply drill a small hole in the channel in which the window slides up and down. This hole should be big enough to accommodate a nail, without having to use too much force to insert or remove it. Drill the hole just below the bottom of the window when it is open; insert the nail, and it won't fall down anymore. Simply remove the nail when you want to shut it. A bigger problem posed by windows such as this is that they let cold air in the house during the winter, increasing your heating bill. You can prevent this by covering the outside of the window with a thick plastic bag secured with duct tape.

Safety First

Here's a really safe way of inspecting your roof for leaks: use binoculars or the zoom lens on your camera. This way, you won't ever have to set foot on the roof, as an accidental fall from up there could be life-threatening. This will also save you money when it comes time to call a repairman, as you will be able to point out to him exactly where the problem is, thereby saving him a great deal of time that would be passed over to you in the bill.

Screen Tips

If the metal screen in your window gets a small tear in it, then you don't have to throw it out. Simply glue the torn area back together with a strong bonding epoxy, which can be found at any hardware store. Always read the directions when using glues such as this. To clean your screen (a chore which should be done at least once a year), hose it down and scrub it with a small piece of shag carpeting.

Ladder Security

The ladder is one of the most important tools you will use while working on the outside of your home; painting the second story of your house is a good example of this. While you should never use a ladder without someone spotting you, here is a tip to make your ladder more stable, in case your spotter gets momentarily distracted. Using strong shears, cut out two pieces, about six inches long each, from that old tire in your garage that you've been meaning to throw out for so long. Take these two strips and nail them to the bottom of each leg of the ladder. This will increase friction, thereby decreasing the chances of the ladder sliding out from under you.

Chapter V:
Laundry

Laundry. The very word itself is depressing. It's that one chore that you will do anything to put off, even to the point of dusting the living room a second time. You hate it because things always go wrong. Colors bleed. Pants and shirts come out wrinkled. Why can't it ever turn out right for once?

Relax! Laundry doesn't have to be your worst nightmare. There are plenty of little things you can do to make it easier and more successful. Just follow the hints below, and you're bound to have far fewer problems. That will be a great relief to you, and you will feel a wonderful sense of satisfaction as you spend some fun afternoons with your family, knowing that the only reason you have this free time is because you now know how to do the wash more quickly!

USE AND CARE OF APPLIANCES

Washing the Washer

Detergents can be harsh on the inside of your washing machine, and after a few months, excessive amounts of residue can build up. To clean out the washer, simply set it on hot and run it empty for an entire cycle. Instead of adding detergent to the water, however, add vinegar. Use the vinegar sparingly and only every now and then, as the acidity could eventually damage the machine.

Clean the Lint Screen

Cleaning the lint screen is the most important regular maintenance you can perform on your dryer. As well as enabling clothes to dry more quickly, thereby saving you money on your utility bills, it can prevent the dryer from getting too hot and catching fire! Simply wiping the lint off each time you use it is not enough. Every week or two you should scrub it with soap and warm water; make sure to rinse well, so no soap builds up on it. Be sure that it is fully dry before replacing it in the machine.

Iron Solid

When you hear the word appliance, then you probably only think of your washer and dryer. But don't forget that your iron is an appliance too, and that you need to take care of it in order to keep it running. When using the mist function on your iron, it is very important that the water is clean! The best water to use is distilled water from bottles, which will leave no deposits whatsoever. Pour out any excess water while the iron is still hot.

Smoothing Scratches

If you are not very careful with your iron, then it is easy to scratch the heating plate. This can be terrible for clothes, creating snags and even tears in fabric, and must be attended to immediately. The solution is to sand down the plate with extra fine grade sandpaper. Your iron won't look so pretty anymore, but it will work just fine. Some scratches may be so deep that the only thing you can do is throw it out.

HOW TO HANDLE CLOTHES

Buy More than One Hamper

Why do most households have just one laundry hamper? Wouldn't it be better to have several, so that everyone can just toss their dirty clothes into the appropriate ones? They can put colors in one, whites in another, etc. If your family is conscientious about this, then you can significantly reduce the amount of time it takes you to do laundry, as you won't have to sort clothes anymore.

Inside Out

One of the most important rules when washing and drying your clothes is to turn them inside out. This will reduce the amount of color that runs, reduce fraying and damage to outer edges, and generally make your clothes last *considerably* longer.

Soap Situation

A lot of people put their clothes in the washer and then pour soap on top. Unless your machine has an agitator (the little dish on top which slowly releases the detergent), this can defeat the whole purpose of doing your laundry. The soap will tend to stay at the top, so only the uppermost clothes in the machine will be properly washed. Instead, you should put the soap in first and add clothes as the washer starts to fill up with sudsy water.

Simply Delicate

Here's a great and inexpensive way to wash your delicate articles of clothing in your washing machine. Simply arrange them inside a pillowcase and tie it shut! There's no hassle to this method whatsoever. You can also use pillow cases in this fashion to clean evenly-shaped jewelry that is not very fragile.

Oily Solutions

Two of the oiliest places on most people's bodies are their neck and wrists. You've probably noticed that your clothes seem to wear out in these spots before anywhere else. To help preserve your clothes and save you the agony of trying to remove stains, encourage your family to wipe these areas with rubbing alcohol prior to dressing.

Iron Now, Not Later

A good way to save time when doing your laundry is to iron immediately after you remove clothes from the dryer. This way, you don't have to separate the clothes twice (once after drying, and then again after ironing). You can also save even more time, because the best time to iron clothes is when they are slightly damp. Turn your dryer off 5 minutes before the timer would normally do, and iron. The ironing itself will complete the drying, and your clothes will be even more wrinkle-free!

Press, Don't Pull

Most people don't realize it, but there are several ways to iron. Any time you are ironing a delicate fabric, or are trying to create a pleat or sharp fold, you should press the garment. This means that rather than pushing and pulling the iron along it, you should press down with the iron in one spot, lift it, and then press down on another spot. Turn clothes inside out when pressing, and use a press cloth when working with delicates.

Aluminum Ironing Board

A great way to speed up ironing is to wrap your ironing board in aluminum foil. Never iron directly onto the aluminum foil, however, as this could be dangerous; always cover the foil with an ironing pad. The foil catches the heat and projects it back upwards, so you virtually iron both sides at once! Most people don't know this, but the two sides of foil are different. Wrap the board in such a way that the shinier side is facing up.

No Wrinkles

It can be really tempting to throw all your clothes in the dryer at once, so that your laundry will be done more quickly. But we all know what happens whenever you do this: your clothes come out wrinkled, even the ones made out of polyester. Then you have to waste an hour or more of your time doing ironing that should not have been necessary. The solution to this is to simply never overload your dryer. If your clothes still come out wrinkled, then try putting a damp towel in with your clothes *once they are already dry*. Turn the dryer on for a few more minutes, and *voila*!

Button Down Solution

Tired of having to struggle to remove clothes from the washer because the sleeves of shirts have gotten wrapped around all the other clothing? Why not simply button the cuffs to the front of the shirt? This idea will save you plenty of time each time you wash a load.

Proper Air

All fabrics are porous materials; as such, like our skin, they need to breathe. Leather is especially sensitive to this, but other fabrics also require fresh air. You should never cover your clothes completely. Remove them from the plastic bags in which dry cleaners put them as soon as you get home. To prevent them from getting dirty, you might want to wrap them in a loose material that is also porous. For example, you can hang a sheet in your closet to cover your entire wardrobe.

Really White

When washing a load of whites, bleach works best if added after the load has been in the machine for a few minutes on the wash cycle. Also, don't be afraid to use really hot water. The key to using temperature successfully is to be careful when separating your clothing; if you know you're going to wash your whites on hot, then don't put any colors in that load.

Where to Put Clothes

This may sound silly, but always put your most recently washed clothing at the back of the closet or on the bottom of the pile of folded clothes. That way, you won't wear these clothes again right away, and they will last longer.

Chapter VI:
Saving Energy, Money, and Lives

You might not want to admit it, but right now you are probably wasting a tremendous amount of energy throughout your house. For example, rather than putting on another layer of clothing, did you turn the heater up? Have you resorted to using the air conditioner when closing the blinds might have cooled down the house?

This chapter will give you a few hints on reducing waste, but it is far from complete. Whole books have been written on this topic. But if you master these basic techniques, then you can congratulate yourself for reducing not just your own utility bills, but the amount of pollution in the world too!

As well as saving the world, you will also learn a little about saving yourself. The few tips presented below can introduce you to the hazards which may be lurking in your household. For example, do you know what kind of items should be kept in a natural disaster survival kit? Do you know how to keep from tripping down the stairs at night when it's dark? You'll soon learn how!

CLIMATE CONTROL

Hot Aluminum

Remember how you learned to use aluminum foil as a kind of "double iron" in the chapter on laundry? Well, the same concept can be used to save energy with heaters. If you place sheets of heavy grade aluminum foil behind your radiator, then you can angle them in such a way as to ensure that more heat is reflected into the room, thereby utilizing the energy more efficiently and saving you money.

The Magic of Blinds

Do you know how a greenhouse works? The concept is very simple: all the panes of glass let rays of light into the structure, which subsequently get trapped inside and raise the temperature. How can you use this greenhouse effect to your advantage? In the summer you should keep your curtains or blinds shut during the day, so that the sunlight will be kept out. That way, you won't have to turn the air conditioning so high. In the winter, you should leave the blinds or curtains open, so that sunlight can enter your house and warm it up. This will reduce your heating bill.

Shut the Door!

This tip is simple yet highly effective. Keep all doors within the house closed while using either air conditioning or heating. This will prevent the warm air or cool air from drifting into unused areas. With the climate control being used more efficiently, you can turn it to a lower setting, thereby saving you money.

WATER CONSERVATION

New Shower Head

One of the greatest new advances in plumbing is the water-conservation shower head. This remarkable new device will save you a considerable amount of money each month by dramatically reducing the amount of water that it sprays. If you're worried that you won't feel as refreshed as you would with a normal shower head, however, then you should lay your fears to rest. By increasing the amount of air that mixes with the water in the spray, you'll hardly notice any difference at all. These heads are even quite inexpensive, and very easy to install!

Not so Tight!

This might surprise you, but one of the worst ways to try and save water is by twisting your faucets very tight when you turn them off. When you do that, all that happens is that you crush the gasket in the faucet, thereby ruining the water tight seal. Over time, the seal deteriorates to such a point that the faucet inevitably becomes leaky, dripping all night long! You'd be amazed at how much a leaky faucet can add to your water bill. So just remember, not too tight.

No Baths, Please

Many people are under the impression that baths use less water than showers, but this couldn't be farther from the truth. If you are conscientious and have quick showers, then you will use much less water. If you find this difficult to believe, then try filling up your bathtub with individual buckets of water; you'll be amazed at how many buckets it takes to fill it up. If you do decide to have a bath, however, there is a way that you can use its energy to your advantage. In winter, when things are chilly, leave the tub filled after having your bath. It will stay relatively hot for about an hour, and this heat will help to raise the temperature of your house!

RECYCLING

Cans and Bottles

If your family goes through lots of soda pop or beer, then you should start saving the used cans and bottles. Whenever convenient, take them to a local supermarket with recycling machines. Recycling not only helps out the environment, it helps out your pocket book too. The redemption value for bottles and cans varies from state to state, but it is usually around a nickel. If you save all of the change that you collect from recycling in a jar, after a few months you'll have enough money to treat your family to something special!

Newspaper

It's wonderful to get the morning paper each day and read it over a hot cup of coffee. But after that, there isn't really any place to put it (if you're like most people, then your garage has a whole year's worth of newspapers stacked up in the corner). Well, now that you're getting your place organized, isn't it about time that you took it to the recycling center at the grocery store? Although not all centers pay you for your used newspaper, at the very least you're getting a pile of junk out of your otherwise neat house. You'll also be helping in the crusade to save the environment, something from which we can all benefit.

Recycled Paper

If you have a home office, then chances are you do a lot of paperwork each day. But instead of using good quality cotton bond paper for every document you produce, why not use recycled white paper whenever you can. Not only is it much cheaper (sometimes you can get it for about one-fiftn the price of bond paper, if you buy ir in bulk!), but it is also much better for the environment. You should at least consider using it for all your rough drafts.

BUDGETING

Plan for the Month

Organizing your bank book is as important as organizing your home. You should set up strict budgets for yourself, and not stray from those budgets. That way, you will force yourself to be on alert for the best bargains. It is probably best to budget out your money for an entire month, rather than for just one week or two. The reason for this is that many items, particularly food and sanitary products, are very cheap when bought in bulk; you will pay much less by buying meat for a month than by buying it for a week. One important category to never leave off of any budget: savings!

Three Months

How much money should you save? This is the question that most people torment themselves with for hours and hours. Many money experts believe that the minimum savings you should have is three months worth of your salary in liquid assets; that is, money that is readily available. Why three months? Let's face it, horrible things can happen at any moment. Three months worth of money should be enough for you to live on if you happen to lose your job, or if you get hospitalized.

Bills

You should keep a file that you go through at least once a week for your bills. You should never leave paying a bill until the last minute, in case your payment gets lost in the mail. Likewise, you shouldn't pay a bill too early, or you will lose the interest on your money that you could have accrued. Try to pay each bill about seven days before it is due. Once you have sent your payment, file the bill in a file just for that type of bill. Then, when it comes time to file your taxes at the end of the year, they will already be sorted into the correct category for you.

Car Care

In this hectic day and age, your car should be considered part of your household. After all, it's just as indispensable as the roof over your head. As such, your household budget should include its maintenance. While such costs vary from car to car, you should be prepared to pay for at least two major servicings per year, two minor servicings (such as oil changes), and at least one regrettable mishap (like needing a new tire). In order to make a good estimate for your car, read your warranty and find out what parts are covered. Ask your dealer for the prices of labor and commonly needed parts that aren't covered.

Be Realistic

The best advice that anyone can get regarding their budget is to be realistic. Don't trick yourself into thinking that a family of four can be fed for $20 a month, because even the best shopper can't find bargains like that. Making a budget that is too tight is like making an impossible New Year's resolution, so save yourself some grief. If anything, you should overestimate your spending; anything that you don't actually spend can go into your savings.

HOME SAFETY

Emergency Kit

Recently, various parts of the country have been ravaged by natural disasters. Whether it's earthquakes in California or flooding along the Mississippi, nature has certainly exerted its dominion over mankind. The key to fighting such disasters is to be prepared. Emergency kits obviously must vary depending upon the disasters that threaten your region of the country; a raft is more important along the Mississippi than it is in Los Angeles, for example. There are certain constants, however. For example, all kits must have radios and flashlights *with fresh batteries*. All kits should have sterile bandages and antiseptics, dried food rations, and several gallons of purified drinking water. Consult emergency officials in your neighborhood for the exact contents necessary in your region. *No house can ever truly be considered organized without an emergency kit.*

Smoke Detectors

Smoke detectors are inexpensive and they can save your life. If you don't already have several in your home, then go out and buy them. If you do already have some in your home, make sure that they are installed correctly and that the batteries are fresh. You should change the batteries at least twice a year. Professionals recommend that you change them when you set your clocks forward or back; that way, you won't forget. Incidentally, that would probably also be a good time to change the batteries in your emergency kit.

Chemicals and Drugs

Kids are naturally curious, and unfortunately they seem to gravitate toward things that aren't good for them. We must all keep hazardous chemicals and prescription drugs around the house, so they must be stored away properly. Always put chemicals, such as cleansing products, on the highest shelves, where they can't be reached by children. You might even want to consider locking them up. You have already learned that drugs should not be stored in the bathroom, so that eliminates the chance of kids finding them in the medicine cabinet. But you shouldn't just leave them lying around in your bedroom, in case your child stumbles upon them; hide them someplace safe!

Sharp Idea
Here's a good way not to cut yourself on the tips of knives that are in drawers: insert them into corks. This will reduce your chance of injury whenever you grab for a knife. This is especially important in households with kids.

Electricity
Have you ever noticed those special electrical outlets they have in hotel bathrooms with the little button on them. This button is a miniature circuit breaker. It cuts the flow of electricity off in the event that you drop a hairdryer or electric shaver into a sink or bathtub filled with water. Most of us aren't lucky enough to have such sophisticated outlets, but we all have fuse boxes in our basements or garages. If you ever drop your hairdryer in the sink, don't touch, or even try to pull the cord out of the wall! Go down and *turn off the fuse corresponding to the outlet in which the appliance is plugged!* Once you have done

this, no more electricity is surging through it, so it is safe to touch. Unplug it, drain the water, and let it dry thoroughly before trying to use it again. An even simpler solution is to always drain the water *before* using a hairdryer or shaver.

Toasted Fingers

Toasters are so easy to use that you probably wouldn't even think twice about letting your youngest child use one. But don't forget, they do carry a large current of energy through them and, as such, can be very dangerous. If a piece of toast ever gets stuck inside, then the first thing you should do is *unplug the appliance*. Then, use a wooden instrument to remove it. Never use your fingers or any metal object, or you run a very high risk of suffering an electrical shock.

Vacation Security

If you are going away on vacation, then you want to make sure your home is safe while you are away. There are professional services which will look after your house, but this can be expensive. Instead, just ask a neighbor to take care of it for you; you will save yourself a lot of money (the only form of payment you might have to make is repaying the favor). Your neighbor should visit your home every day and turn different lights on and off. He or she should open the curtains in the morning and close them at night. He or she should collect your mail and your newspaper, and possibly even take care of your lawn. The idea is to make sure that no burglar would ever suspect that your house is empty.

Burned Batteries

We all know the feeling of reaching for a flashlight and turning it on . . . only to find that nothing happens. When you open it up, you discover that the batteries are so old that they've actually started to melt and the acid is dripping out, destroying the inside of your flashlight. There is no way to prevent this from happening to any battery operated appliance. The only thing you can do is change your batteries on a regular basis, so that nothing gets damaged and everything functions when needed.

Stair Cases

Stair cases can be remarkably dangerous, especially to kids and the elderly. You should always do your best to draw attention to the first and last steps of any staircase, so that eyes cannot be distracted away from them, especially in dark places. Cover the first and last steps of your cellar stair case with fluorescent tape.

Glass

We all keep a great deal of glass products in the kitchen and bathroom. Unfortunately, these types of rooms usually have hard tile floors, meaning that if anything made of glass gets dropped, then it will probably break. Those tiny little shards are so hard to find! To make your search easier, turn off the main lights and shine a flashlight on the ground. The shards will identify themselves by reflecting the flashlight beam.

No More Bacteria

Bacteria can be one of the most dangerous threats in your house. But if you know how to handle foods correctly, then you need not worry. Firstly, you should clean your can opener thoroughly at least once a week. Don't just wash it off with water, but scrub it with baking soda. Secondly, if you ever open a can and hear a loud hissing noise, then *throw out the contents of the can immediately! They have been tainted while still on the shelf!* Finally, in the event of a power outage, never open your refrigerator or freezer to make sure your food is okay. If you leave them shut, then they will not start warming up for several hours, which is usually enough time for the electricity to return. If, however, the power takes a long time to come back and your frozen foods thaw out, then you will have to throw them out. Never refreeze them.

Bright Ideas

You always seem to forget where you put the flashlight when there's a power outage. A good way to help you find useful items such as these in the dark is to wrap them in fluorescent tape. This can also be helpful on light switches and light cords if you have to get up suddenly in the middle of the night. Also, if a fuse ever blows, have a spare one already attached to the side of the box with tape, so that you'll always be able to turn the lights back on in a jiffy.

Chapter VII:
Hiring Help

People are finally starting to realize that organizing and managing a household is a difficult task. This task can take many hours out of your day, and when it is done best, people don't notice that it has been done at all. As such, at some point in your task of creating a well organized household, you may have to ask yourself if you need help.

At first you should try to recruit this help from family members and friends. Ask everyone to pitch in and do their fair share. Kids should not be excused from this duty, as they often feel a sense of pride at being invited to join in on "adult" activities. Besides, there's more than enough work to go around.

If you still feel that you need help, then you will probably have to hire someone. But this is an important decision, not to be taken lightly, for you are asking a stranger to come into your house. What measures can you take to find the most efficient, most trustworthy, and best qualified person for the job? This chapter will show you how to do so. Relax, because it is not as difficult as it sounds.

CHOOSING

Should I, Shouldn't I?

Hiring an outsider is one of the biggest organizational decisions you will have to make regarding your home. While this person may be a tremendous help with chores and watching your children, what if you feel like your home has been intruded? In the first place, you're the boss, so don't hire anyone with whom you are not entirely comfortable. In the second place, many families legitimately *need* outside help these days; it's getting harder and harder to raise a family on just one income.

Where Should I Go to Find Help?

There are certainly many fine agencies who can match you with a helper. They have candidates specially trained as cleaners, sitters, cooks, companions (for the sick and elderly), drivers, etc. If you need one person for a specific duty, then an agency may be appropriate for you. Simply look one up in the yellow pages. But if you need more generalized help, then why not try placing an ad at the local university job center? There are plenty of stu-

113

dents who would love to supplement their income by returning to a "homey" environment.

The Right Person

Don't forget that you are the boss, and you have the right to choose the best person for the job. Ask questions — lots of questions. That's what "real" employers do when they interview people for a job, so why shouldn't you? You have the right to know whether or not your new employee smokes, has a work permit, has special skills, likes kids, etc. Be wary of people who simply need a place to live while settling into a new neighborhood.

Credentials

No matter how you decide to get help, always ask for references. You want someone trustworthy in your home, and no one can be trusted so implicitly if they can't even provide you with the names and numbers of three employers, teachers, or other upstanding members of the community. Also, try to find someone with related experience or a good track record. For example, if you want someone to watch your kids, then perhaps look for a student who is majoring in education. Or if you want a driver, find someone whose DMV record is clean.

Reference Questions

So you've asked your prospective employee for references, and you are about to call those people on the phone, but you suddenly realize that you don't know what you're supposed to ask. Just ask for the truth. How do you know this person? Is this person trustworthy and reliable? What is this person's best quality? What is this person's worst quality? Were you happy with this person's work (ask this to a teacher or former employer, not a personal reference)? If the reference senses that you simply want honest answers, then chances are they will provide them.

PAYMENT

In and Out

The two major classifications of hired help are those who live in and those who live out. Live in help is usually much cheaper, as most of the salary takes the form of room and board, but you lose considerably more of your privacy. This kind of help is often best reserved for sitters for young children or other jobs where 24-hour assistance could be needed. Hired help who lives out can be paid up to about three or four times as much as their live in counterparts, but you do not have to worry about feeding them or providing them with a room.

How Much?

It can be a difficult decision deciding how much you are willing to pay your help. No matter what duties they fulfill, however, a good rule of thumb is to consider any special circumstances. For example, do you have an unusually large family (for sitters), is your house particularly big (for cleaners), is it far away from town (for drivers), and do you need someone to put in extra-long days? If your answer to any of these questions, or to any similar questions, is yes, then you're going to have to offer more money. Your help should be paid every week.

Food Facts

While you cannot consider food a legitimate form of reimbursement, you should be willing to provide your employee with meals when they work. And these should be nice meals, just like the rest of the family eats. It is not adequate or fair for you to feed your help leftovers (especially if your employee is the cook!). Give your employee free access to the refrigerator, but make sure that he or she does not abuse this right. It is only natural that a well fed employee will work better.

Other Compensation

If your employee lives outside your home, then you should be prepared to pay for his or her bus fare. If he or she has a car, then pay for gas (this is especially true if you are hiring this person to run errands — in that case, you need to develop a system of monitoring gas consumption so that you are not cheated). If your employee lives in your house, then provide a nice room for him or her. The room should be welcoming, not foreboding. Have a nice little table and a nice little TV. Make sure the bed is comfortable. While this may not be your employee's home *per se*, it is not fair for you to make him or her live in uncomfortable conditions.

Taxes

Whenever you hire anyone, you have to take into account taxes. Are you going to pay their annual withholdings or are they going to have to take care of that themselves? You might also want to consider different insurance plans, such as Workman's Compensation. Contact your accountant or local Chamber of Commerce for information about these types of issues.

Budgeting

In the previous chapter, you learned a few tips about how to budget your income. If you wish to hire outside help, then naturally your budget is going to have to reflect this. Once again, be realistic about the amount of money you would need to spend hiring someone. Perhaps this is simply out of your budget. If you do have some money, but not a lot, then you can always "sweeten the deal" that you offer; how about one paid day off every month, for example? Also, remember that the more you can take care of yourself, the less time you will need someone working in your home; thus, if you personally are able to follow as many of the suggestions in this book as possible, then maybe you can hire someone part-time instead of full-time.

RULES AND TRAINING

Friends and Neighbors

If you have hired someone to work in your home, then you're going to have to give them some of the rights of anyone else in the household. Allow him or her to use the phone. Allow him or her to have friends over occasionally. Allow him or her to make slight changes in the schedule, if absolutely necessary. The key here is to lay down some strict ground rules. For example, no long distance calls before 5:00 p.m. Or no guests before noon.

Family Food

Don't make your employee guess what you like to eat. If this person is going to cook for you, then provide clear recipes. You should even go to the grocery store with him or her to make sure that they know how to find the best bargains and do not buy any brands that you do not like. It is within your rights to demand that your employee is a good cook, but you have to show that person what you consider good cooking. And it is always a nice gesture to budget a certain amount each week for foods that he or she likes.

Healthy?

It is not unreasonable to ask your new employee to get a check up. After all, you don't want anyone playing with your children who doesn't have a clean bill of health. But, you must understand that it is your responsibility to pay for such a check up, and there are certain personal matters that the employee has the right to keep to himself or herself.

Training

All new employees need training, no matter what the job, and hiring someone to help you out in your home can be very frustrating for *them*. Perhaps, for example, you don't keep the cleaning supplies where they naturally would. As such, you should give them a little bit of freedom to reorganize things within reason; this will make them more efficient in the long run. You are going to have to spend several days going over their duties with them. Watch them as they work and suggest changes as the need arises. Don't burden them with too many duties at once; perhaps show them four or five new things a day, and by the end of the first week they should have a solid idea of what is expected of them. Encourage them to ask questions. After about a month, your household should be in a routine, but try to be understanding if your employee doesn't know how to deal with every new situation. For example, perhaps he or she does not know that the outside faucets must be turned off when it starts getting cold at the end of autumn.

Outside Training

If training seems like a difficult task to you, then you are not alone. It is only when you are faced with the challenge of showing someone how to do something that you really start to understand just how difficult teaching is. One of the benefits of hiring through a professional service is that the employees are all trained by the agency. As such, they merely need to learn the idiosyncrasies of your particular home. The amount of time it takes them to learn the ropes should therefore be fairly swift.

Conclusion

Congratulations! You can pat yourself on the back, because you now know how to make your house a more organized home!

If you follow even just a few of the suggestions discussed throughout this book, then your house will be more efficient, safer, and more pleasant. Your clothes will smell fresher. Your yard will look neater. Even your food might taste better. That's quite an accomplishment, after reading just one book.

Chances are, after you've seen how a few of these hints can save you quite a bit of time and money, you'll want to try out more of them in your home. Hopefully, you will adopt as many as you can, constantly striving to make your home a more comfortable place. And after you've completed the initial transition of reorganization, things will go much more smoothly and quickly, giving you more free time then you ever thought possible.

Enjoy the time and money you will save. Use it to pamper yourself and your loved ones.

Good luck!

Notes

Notes

Notes